101 ideas
to energize youth ministry volunteers

by
Kurt Johnston and Katie Edwards

Loveland, Colorado

Dedication

"This book is dedicated to our incredible families. Ron and Abby Edwards and Rachel, Kayla, and Cole Johnston...you are our most important teammates!"

101 Ideas to Energize Youth Ministry Volunteers
Copyright © 2004 Kurt Johnston and Katie Edwards

Visit our Web site: www.grouppublishing.com

Credits
Editor: Kelli B. Trujillo
Creative Development Editor: Dave Thornton
Chief Creative Officer: Joani Schultz
Copy Editor: Patty Wyrick
Book Art Direction and Production: Nathan Hindman
Cover Art Director: Jeff A. Storm
Cover Designer and Book Illustrator: Toolbox Creative
Production Manager: Dodie Tipton

Unless otherwise noted, Scripture taken from the HOLY BIBLE, NEW INTERNATIONAL VERSION®. Copyright © 1973, 1978, 1984 by International Bible Society. Used by permission of Zondervan Publishing House. All rights reserved.

Library of Congress Cataloging-in-Publication Data
Johnston, Kurt, 1966–
    Go team! : 101 ideas to energize youth ministry volunteers / by Kurt Johnston and Katie Edwards.
       p.   cm.
Includes bibliographical references.
ISBN 0-7644-2650-8 (pbk. : alk. paper)
1. Church work with youth. 2. Voluntarism--Religious aspects--Christianity. I. Edwards, Katie, 1974- II. Title.
    BV4447 .J54 2004
    259' .23--dc22
                                                            2004002942

10 9 8 7 6 5 4 3 2 1   13 12 11 10 09 08 07 06 05 04
Printed in the United States of America.

CONTENTS

FOREWORD

Over my youth ministry career, I've had the privilege of writing and endorsing many books. But I'm not sure I've ever been part of a book where I smiled during every page. My affection for this book rests on several layers:

(1) I love the authors! They are friends, colleagues, and ministers who have personally impacted me and the lives of my own teenagers;

(2) I love volunteers! Healthy youth ministry can't happen without a foundation of men and women who give up their time to love teenagers and point them to Jesus; and

(3) I love ideas! This book is filled with them. I've seen many of these ideas used firsthand with the volunteers at Saddleback Church. With the ideas that I haven't seen used, I found myself smiling and saying, "That's a great idea...I bet you that was Katie's. Or that's funny...it sounds so much like Kurt!" These two friends are fun, kind, Christlike, and encouraging, and this helpful book of ideas will be a refreshing addition to a youth worker's tool kit! Actually, if you implement just one idea, you'll get your money's worth from this book. But be wise and use them all.

Those of us who work with volunteers often commit the crime of recruiting adults to help in the youth ministry and then leaving them to figure it out on their own. We recruit and then run to our next task (which is often to recruit more help). As a youth worker, I know this is both true and understandable. (I've done it many times.) And if I've described you, don't feel guilty—just don't continue in that pattern. When we recruit and run, we do so believing that the new volunteers will survive and *surely* understand why we had to turn our backs on them—we had more to do. Then, when a volunteer dries up and quits our youth ministry, we wonder what went wrong. But before we learn from our mistake, we rush out to find a replacement volunteer without considering what just happened.

What <u>did</u> just happen? When volunteers don't receive encouragement for their efforts, their emotional tanks will empty. Youth ministry is draining. Teenagers aren't exactly the most affirming human beings, and when the normal youth ministry stuff appears, discouragement is unavoidable. It's at this point when volunteers decide that sharpening the little pencils in the pews might be a more rewarding ministry than working with teenagers.

When a volunteer quits, the resignation impacts the culture of youth ministry in your church. The revolving door of youth workers creates an atmosphere where students don't know who's coming, who's going, or who to trust. Within this changing culture, it's understandable that a fourteen-year-old won't open up to a volunteer leader after four other "caring" volunteers have already come in and out of her life in the last two years. Because she's unlikely to trust the new adult, she has the potential to be spiritually damaged. When this happens, the youth ministry is damaged and the church is damaged. It's an ugly, painful reality.

Why do most volunteers quit? My experience has been that adults leave the ministry because they are underappreciated and feel little value. Thankfully, this book will help you break the negative cycle of abusing and losing volunteer leaders by finding fun and creative ways to value and appreciate them. You hold in your hands a book full of practical, proven, and fun ideas that should help the revolving-door reality change. My twenty-five-plus years in youth ministry have shown me that when volunteers stick around, they become more effective ministers. Longevity equals effectiveness.

I have watched Kurt and Katie keep volunteers around for a long time. Caring adults join their team because they want to serve, but they stay on their team because they are encouraged, equipped, and empowered. I can't even count how many times I've wanted junior high volunteers to move up with a graduating junior high class but the volunteers have refused! Their refusal isn't a personal reaction against the high school ministry I oversee; it's personal because of the junior high ministry. These leaders feel loved, valued, and honored, and they want to continue to minister in that environment. Do you blame them? I don't.

Kurt and Katie are not simply idea-writers who wrote these thoughts in isolation. These ideas have been created and used within the youth ministry at Saddleback Church, and our volunteers have been the lucky recipients. Not only am I thankful as a youth worker for these great ideas, but I'm also very grateful as a father whose own children love the church because of the junior high leaders in their lives. My kids don't love coming to church because of the programs; they love it because of the people. That's good youth ministry and one that I'm proud to send my kids to!

Everyone needs encouragement, especially those of us who work with teenagers.

DOUG FIELDS

INTRODUCTION

Volunteers change lives. At youth group meetings, in Sunday school, at summer camp, during pizza parties, on retreats, in small groups, during lock-ins, and in countless other ways, volunteers are making an incredible difference in the lives of the young people in your student ministry.

Ministry is about teamwork, and the volunteers in your church are the most important members of your team! Let's face it, without volunteers using their gifts and sacrificing their time, the local church would be very ineffective.

Unfortunately, many volunteers feel worn out, underappreciated, and ready to throw in the towel. We've learned this the hard way. Volunteers in our ministry have fizzled out, burned out, walked out, and even cussed us out! Perhaps you've had similar experiences.

There are several factors that contribute to your ministry's ability to keep volunteers involved for the long haul. Getting the right volunteers to start with, providing them ongoing training, giving them clear expectations and direction, and providing healthy leadership are all very important. However, the most important thing you can do for your volunteers is oftentimes overlooked or underestimated: *Encourage them!* The little, simple things you say and do to encourage and support your volunteers really do make a big difference.

You've probably never heard a volunteer in your ministry say, "Please stop encouraging me" or "I feel like you support me too much." In fact, if they were totally honest, many volunteers would admit to feeling like they don't get the support and encouragement they need from the leadership of the church.

That's why this book was written! We want to help you keep the volunteer leaders God has given your ministry by giving you a whole bunch of tried and true ideas to encourage and energize your volunteer team. You won't find the newest recruiting methods or impressive leadership training outlines here. Instead, we're simply giving you over a hundred fun, simple ideas that you can use in your setting to encourage your volunteers and let them know how valuable they are to your ministry.

A Few Tips

First, recognize your own ministry setting. We happen to work in a junior high ministry, but most of these ideas will transfer into almost any ministry setting—*almost* any setting. If you work with a group of 65-year-old ladies who volunteer their time stuffing your weekend bulletin, they may not be encouraged by being invited to your "Macho Movies" night.

Second, pace yourself. It's easy to grab a book like this and start going a little overboard. Pick and choose what ideas will work best, and be strategic in your timing. Like we said before, nobody has ever heard that a ministry leader is too encouraging, but if you aren't careful, this book may make *you* the first!

Third, customize. You know your ministry better than we do, and you are probably more creative than we are. Take these ideas and make them even better by adding a personal touch wherever needed.

Finally, share this book! In a few months, your volunteers will feel so encouraged that they will begin talking to other people who will begin talking to other people who will begin talking to other leaders in your church who will feel the need to encourage their volunteers—and pretty soon everybody who volunteers in your church will be encouraged, refreshed, and ready to change the world. (This is a slight exaggeration, but they *will* be ready to change another diaper in the nursery!) But that amazing scenario can only happen if you pass this book around. Everyone in your church who works with volunteers can benefit from the ideas we've included. Passing the book around is great. An *even better* idea is to let them buy their own copy!

What You'll Find

This book is organized in nine themed sections so you can find ideas that will fit your specific needs. Each idea includes a list of the necessary supplies, the estimated cost, and a simple description of how to pull it off. In addition to these tried-and-true encouragement ideas, you'll find

- *Essays* about the ins and outs of working with volunteers,

- *Team Talk* testimonials from volunteers who are a part of our youth ministry team at Saddleback, and

- *Top 5* lists that will help you laugh about the ups and downs of volunteer ministry.

Your volunteers play a key role in helping teenagers develop relationships with each other and, more importantly, with Jesus. As your volunteers feel affirmed and empowered, their spiritual impact in the lives of students will grow exponentially. As you browse through these pages, our prayer is that God will give you a new, fresh desire to encourage and support the volunteers in your ministry like never before...because volunteers really do *change lives.*

GET CREATIVE!

The best part of encouraging and energizing volunteers is coming up with new and creative methods of affirmation. Over the years, we've had a few ideas that just didn't work (like the time we tried to mail bowling balls), but the truth is, just about any encouragement idea is a good idea. We've decided to begin the book by sharing a few creative ideas that did work...most of the time.

1. SPECIAL DELIVERY

SUPPLIES NEEDED: candy bar, padded envelope, note card, postage

COST: under $3 per person

Everyone loves mail! Find out what your volunteer's favorite candy bar is, and send it to him or her in the mail. Mail it in an envelope, or stick the address label and the stamp right on the candy bar! Attach a note of encouragement on the back side of the candy bar.

EXAMPLE

"You are doing an awesome job as a small group leader. Take a break today, kick your feet up, and enjoy a treat on us! Have a sweet day!"

TIP

Take the candy bar to the post office to have it weighed so you get the correct postage. You also might want to purchase a candy bar that won't easily melt: for example, a Starburst or PayDay (although this could be tough since most people enjoy chocolate)!

2. EXTRA! EXTRA! READ ALL ABOUT IT!

SUPPLIES NEEDED: none

COST: under $5 per person

A unique way to encourage a volunteer is to take out a "Thank You" ad in the local classifieds. Check out your local community newspaper, and place your thank you note in the section that has all of the announcements. For a small fee, you can take out an advertisement thanking an individual or the entire team. You can also have the ad run in the paper for a couple of weeks, just to make sure that everyone on your team

FIRST CHURCH VOLUNTEERS

Thank you for all the hard work on our camp fundraiser. Because of your sacrifice, we were able to take 25 students to camp!

sees it. After you place the ad, send your volunteer an e-mail telling him or her to check out the local paper, or cut the ad out and send it to that person. Either way, it's a cool way to say thanks.

3. SOUND BITES

SUPPLIES NEEDED: blank video, cassette, or CD; group of people to record message; video camera

COST: under $5 per person

Get a group of students, parents, church staff, or fellow volunteers together, and create a sound bite of encouragement. Make a video or record an audio tape for your special volunteer. You can have them record a number of encouraging bits and pieces. Play the tape at your weekly meeting, mail it, or drop it by the office. Either way, it's an awesome encouragement and keepsake.

EXAMPLES

Try recording...
- *people saying "thank you."*
- *someone telling the story of a funny memory.*
- *a group saying thank you all at once.*
- *people talking about what qualities make that person a great part of the team.*
- *a student talking about the impact that person has had.*
- *a joke that will make the volunteer laugh.*
- *a video clip of the volunteer in action with students.*
- *the pastor saying thank you for what the volunteer is doing.*

4. SINGING TELEGRAM

SUPPLIES NEEDED: none
COST: free

Have students show up on the front door of your volunteer's house and deliver a special "Singing Telegram." This is perfect for birthdays, anniversaries, or any celebration, but it's also a fun way to surprise your volunteer for no reason at all. You may want to write a fun jingle that students can easily memorize so you can use the same song each time. Or find out your volunteer's favorite band, and have students sing a medley of cover songs!

EXAMPLES

- *Remember that '80s hit "She Works Hard for the Money"? Sing a spoof of it or any other catchy tune that will have your volunteer smiling and humming all day.*

- *Use familiar nursery-song melodies, such as "Old MacDonald," "This Old Man," or "The Farmer in the Dell," and write new lyrics. For example, students could sing this to the tune of "The Farmer in the Dell": "A big thank you to you, a big thank you to you, a big thank you to (person's name), a big thank you to you!"*

- *Find out from a volunteer's spouse or friend what that person's favorite genre of music or current song is. Then simply write a goofy spoof of that song!*

TIP

Have the students dress up in silly costumes as they sing to your volunteer. The more mismatched and funky, the better! If the students sing a cover tune, have them dress up as the band.

5. COUPONS!

SUPPLIES NEEDED: colored paper, sample coupons
COST: free

Make a fun book full of creative coupons as a thank-you to volunteers. Find people in your church who would be willing to honor each category or donate services to the book. Then create your own unique coupons! Clip out a coupon from the newspaper, and model your coupons after the real thing. This coupon book is a great way to say thank you at the end of a school year or at the end of a long project.

EXAMPLES

- *good for one free lawn mowing*
- *good for one free haircut*
- *good for one free house cleaning*
- *good for one free night of baby-sitting*
- *good for one free dinner (Have someone bring a meal.)*
- *good for one free movie rental (Attach a gift certificate.)*
- *good for one day of chauffeur service to and from work*
- *good for one free car wash*

TIP

Throw in a gift certificate or a few real coupons to local places. For example, throw in a two-for-one coupon to a local restaurant.

6. BRAG TO THE BOSS

SUPPLIES NEEDED: none
COST: free

If it's appropriate, call a volunteer's boss to "brag on them." Call or e-mail that person's boss and in a very short, articulate manner, share with him or her the impact the employee is making in the community, in families, and in the lives of students after work hours as a volunteer. Companies love knowing that their employees are having influence in the community and often give out perks and rewards as a result.

7. VOLUNTEER SUNDAY

SUPPLIES NEEDED: varies
COST: varies

Many churches have set aside one Sunday a year to emphasize certain things such as missions, youth ministry, special programs, and so on. Encourage your pastor to set aside a Sunday to emphasize the importance of volunteer ministry and to thank those who are volunteering in various ways. There are a number of ways to enhance this special day.

EXAMPLES
- *Create a Ministry Fair that highlights the opportunities to volunteer.*
- *Make a video to play during the service that shows volunteers in action.*
- *Have all volunteers stand up during the church service, and give them a small gift.*
- *Ask the pastor or elders to pray over them.*
- *Ask key volunteers to share a personal story of what their ministry has meant to them.*
- *Have a "thank-you" luncheon or reception for all volunteers.*

8. STOLEN CAR

SUPPLIES NEEDED: note card, candy, car keys
COST: under $15 per person

The word *theft* is probably not the first word that comes to mind when you are thinking of encouraging a volunteer, but trust us—they will love this kind of encouragement! Get an extra set of car keys from a parent or spouse. While the volunteer is at work, steal his or her car and get it professionally washed and vacuumed. Return it with a little note of thanks and candy on the seat. Be sure to double-check your volunteer's schedule...you don't want to leave your friend stranded at a location without a car!

TIP

Call your local carwash, and see if the owner is willing to donate a few free car washes. Tell the owner what you are doing and why. It never hurts to ask!

EXAMPLE

"Thanks for always staying late to clean up after students in the youth room on Wednesday nights. We thought we would return the favor! Thanks for your ministry and your time. Have a great day!"

9. VOLUNTEER OF THE MONTH

SUPPLIES NEEDED: picture of your volunteer with students
COST: free

Highlight volunteers in your church bulletin or on your church Web site. Find a picture of your volunteer with students or with other volunteers, and write a short article about that person. End the article with a personal thank-you note to your volunteer.

EXAMPLE

Ron Edwards has been a faithful volunteer in the youth ministry for ten years. He has a huge heart for students and has been involved with leading small groups, being a camp counselor, and teaching at our weekend program. His current ministry with students is teaching a two-hour study on Creation vs. Evolution. Thank you, Ron, for all of your hard work in our ministry. We know you love what you do, and we appreciate your heart for students!

TIP

Try to get a picture of your volunteer "in the trenches" with students. The picture will be a wonderful memory for your volunteer, but it will also serve as an awesome advertisement to the rest of the church family. It might inspire others to check out serving in your ministry.

10. CAN YOU HEAR ME NOW?

SUPPLIES NEEDED: none
COST: free

Leave a message on your volunteer's cell phone, or send him or her a text message in the middle of the day. (You can also leave a message on that person's home answering machine or send a quick e-mail.) This is a great way to encourage volunteers when you don't have a lot of time on your hands or when you are traveling. It's an easy way to let volunteers know that you are thinking about them.

11. MINTY FRESH

SUPPLIES NEEDED: note card, postcard, or self-stick note; hanging car freshener
COST: under $2 per person

Attach an inspirational Scripture or encouraging note to a car freshener that hangs on the rearview mirror in the car. You can mail it out, hand deliver it, or ask a volunteer's spouse to sneak into the car and hang it as a surprise.

EXAMPLE
"Sue, thanks for the fresh ideas you shared at our last meeting!"

DEEPER SUPPORT

This book is dedicated to providing you with a bunch of fun, creative ways to encourage and energize your team. However, it's important to recognize that your volunteers also need ongoing support at a deeper level.

Pray for them. Sounds like a no-brainer, doesn't it? Unfortunately, our greatest source of encouragement is often forgotten or pushed aside because of other pressing needs. What better way to encourage your team than to lift them up regularly and individually before our heavenly Father?

Spend one-on-one time with them. Get some time with each leader alone once in a while. Take this time to ask him or her below-the-surface questions, such as "How's your marriage doing?" "How can I pray for you today?" "What has God been teaching you?" or "How have you grown in your faith lately?"

It's easy to assume that all of our volunteers already have someone in their lives who is giving them the deeper support that we all need, but that just isn't true. Your role as the leader in your ministry is to chart the course and cast the vision, but it's *also* to be a shepherd to the volunteers in your flock. Deeper support doesn't come easy. It's tough work, it takes time, and it can get messy at times...but it's worth it.

12. GET WELL

SUPPLIES NEEDED: any first-aid supply (such as adhesive or elastic bandages), note card, envelope, postage
COST: under $3 per person

Unfortunately, injuries can sometimes occur during youth events...and it's not always the students that get hurt. If one of your volunteers gets hurt "in the line of duty," send that person a cool get-well card using any first-aid supply. For example, unroll an elastic bandage and write a get-well note on the inside. Roll up the completed note, and send it to your volunteer with instructions to unwrap!

EXAMPLE

"Hope you are feeling better! Thanks for putting yourself in harm's way for the kids! You are awesome!"

13. Mr. Clean

Supplies Needed: sponge, scouring pad, or bar of soap; note card or sticky label; envelope; postage

Cost: under $2 per person

Do you have volunteers who stay late to clean up after events? Cleaning up after students has got to be the most thankless job in youth ministry. For those special volunteers who stay late to clean up, send a bar of soap or a scouring pad with a note attached. It's a job that not many people love to do, so take time out to encourage and appreciate them.

14. Tee Time or Tea Time

Supplies Needed: varies

Cost: varies

Send male volunteers a golf tee with an invite to play a round of golf attached. Send female volunteers a tea bag with an invite for tea. Afterwards, meet in the middle somewhere for a group activity. For example, have everyone meet at the church for a game night and dinner after their separate activities.

Ideas for Tee Time

- *Go to a regulation golf course, break into groups, and hack away! Give silly awards for most trees hit, shortest drive, and so on.*
- *Go to a miniature golf course. This makes it fun for everyone—golfers and nongolfers alike. Give prizes for each hole-in-one. Encourage the guys to come dressed in tacky golf clothes.*
- *Rent a fun golf video game, and have everyone meet at the home of someone with a big-screen television. Even grown-ups enjoy a fun video game from time to time!*

Ideas for Tea Time

- *Call a tea shop, and ask what they serve for tea. Use their ideas!*
- *Find people to serve the ladies.*
- *Get a teapot or a teacup for each volunteer to take home.*
- *Have fancy old hats, gloves, and scarves for the ladies to wear. Or have each lady come dressed in "Grandma's best."*
- *Have the tea party in someone's garden.*

15. Scripture Lifter: Two Are Better Than One

Supplies Needed: a small piece of rope, note card
Cost: under $2 per person

Youth ministry has a way of feeling overwhelming at times. There is just so much to do, and it seems like the job never ends! Ecclesiastes 4:12 is a great reminder and encouragement to those volunteers who feel alone or discouraged. Write an encouragement note including Ecclesiastes 4:12, "Though one may be overpowered, two can defend themselves. A cord of three strands is not quickly broken." Attach it to a strong piece of braided rope. It's just a small reminder that together, with God's help, we can make it!

16. Scripture Lifter: God Is My Rock

Supplies Needed: a small rock, note card
Cost: free (Look in your back yard.)

Youth ministry can also be a little bit intimidating at times. Volunteers can sometimes think they are too old or not cool enough to reach today's youth. At times they feel like they are not equipped to be youth ministry volunteers. Find a small rock and attach Isaiah 41:10: "So do not fear, for I am with you; do not be dismayed, for I am your God." Remind your volunteers to lean on God's strength through the thick and thin of ministry. God is the "rock" and the center of ministry. He will guide them through anything!

17. Scripture Lifter: Slow to Grow

Supplies Needed: small potted plant, sticky label or note card
Cost: under $5 per person

Find a small potted plant, and attach the text of James 5:7-11 to the side of the pot. It's a great reminder to your volunteers to be patient, stand firm, and trust God with their ministry. Even if your friend doesn't see progress right away, God is still working in his or her life and in the lives of students. Blessed are those who persevere and follow God's lead.

"Be patient, then, brothers, until the Lord's coming. See how the farmer waits for the land to yield its valuable crop and how patient he is for the autumn and spring rains. You too, be patient and stand firm, because the Lord's coming is near. Don't grumble against each other, brothers, or you will be judged. The Judge is standing at the door! Brothers, as an example of patience in the face of suffering, take the prophets who spoke in the name of the Lord. As you know, we consider blessed those who have persevered. You have heard of Job's perseverance and have seen what the Lord finally brought about. The Lord is full of compassion and mercy" (James 5:7-11).

18. SCRIPTURE LIFTER: WASHED UP

SUPPLIES NEEDED: bar of soap, hand towel, note card
COST: under $5 per person

Volunteers are a great picture of servant leadership! In a real sense, they are washing the feet of others by giving their time and talents. Let them know you recognize this by giving them a small bar of soap or a hand towel and attaching the following Scripture: "So he got up from the meal, took off his outer clothing, and wrapped a towel around his waist. After

that, he poured water into a basin and began to wash his disciples' feet, drying them with the towel that was wrapped around him. He came to Simon Peter, who said to him, 'Lord, are you going to wash my feet?' Jesus replied, 'You do not realize now what I am doing, but later you will understand.' 'No,' said Peter, 'you shall never wash my feet.' Jesus answered, 'Unless I wash you, you have no part with me' " (John 13:4-8).

Include a short note thanking the volunteer for washing the feet of others through his or her commitment to student ministry.

TEAM TALK

"Encouragement is something that has been given freely and in much abundance since I have been serving in our junior high ministry. When I started serving, I was a senior in high school and felt like I had all the time in the world. When I made the transition into college, it was nice to know that the junior high staff could recognize where my heart was. I wanted to continue to serve where needed in junior high but realized that it was going to take a lot of hard work in order to maintain a balance between college life and ministry. My spirits were kept high by full support from the staff that is really more like a family. I could clearly see that I was a valued part of ministry. It was made clear to me that I was not just another volunteer but an important part of a ministry and a team."

—Ryanne Dearden
College student; junior high small group leader; loves to laugh

19. Scripture Lifter: Feeling Sheepish

Supplies Needed: a small piece of wool, note card, envelope, postage
Cost: under $2 per person

Another great picture of the role of a volunteer is that of a shepherd. In short, youth ministry is watching over, feeding, and protecting a flock of students. Find a small piece of sheep's wool or a picture of a shepherd with sheep and attach John 10:11: "I am the good shepherd. The good shepherd lays down his life for the sheep." You can hand deliver it or drop it in the mail. It's a great picture of the role a youth ministry volunteer is playing.

20. Scripture Lifter: A Piece of the Puzzle

Supplies Needed: construction paper or cardboard, black marker, envelope, postage
Cost: under $1 per person

Let's face it—ministry can be a puzzling task! Get a piece of construction paper, and write in big bold letters, "Luke 1:37: 'For nothing is impossible with God.'" Cut the paper into eight pieces, creating a mini jigsaw puzzle with the verse. Send it to a volunteer who needs some encouraging words.

TIP

Most craft stores have blank cardboard puzzles that you can use to make a custom puzzle.

21. Scripture Lifter: Time Out

Supplies Needed: large note card, black marker, envelope, postage
Cost: under $1 per person

It's easy to get so busy doing God's work that we forget about God all together! At times you may need to remind your volunteers to slow down and spend a moment in awe of their heavenly Father like the psalmist did in Psalm 100: "Shout for joy to the Lord, all the earth. Worship the Lord with gladness; come before him with joyful songs. Know that the Lord is

God. It is he who made us, and we are his; we are his people, the sheep of his pasture. Enter his gates with thanksgiving and his courts with praise; give thanks to him and praise his name. For the Lord is good and his love endures forever; his faithfulness continues through all generations."

Write "Time Out" in bold letters on the front of a card, and on the back encourage your friend to take a five-minute timeout during the day to praise God for his blessings in that person's life. Encourage the volunteer to check out Psalm 100.

22. SCRIPTURE LIFTER: A MOMENT OF PEACE

SUPPLIES NEEDED: note card, peaceful item, envelope, postage
COST: varies

Volunteering to work with students can be a draining task at times. Take a moment to remind volunteers to draw strength from God when they are in seasons of weariness.

Grab a tea bag, a picture of something peaceful, or a soothing music CD, and put it together with Matthew 11:28-30: "Come to me, all you who are weary and burdened, and I will give you rest. Take my yoke upon you and learn from me, for I am gentle and humble in heart, and you will find rest for your souls. For my yoke is easy and my burden is light." It's a great reminder for your volunteers to find rest in the Lord at all times.

PILE ON THE PRAISE, NOT THE PRESSURE!

There are a few things that make me (Kurt) really sad: when the Denver Broncos lose, when the Oakland Raiders win, and when a volunteer in our ministry feels overworked and underappreciated. A common but understandable mistake ministry leaders make is to lock in on and overuse those volunteers who have proven themselves willing, ready, and able to tackle just about any job we throw their way. This works great in the short term. Such volunteers say yes to one more request, and the job gets done well with minimal effort on your part. It seems great. They love you and your ministry and will do anything for it. You love them and their commitment to your ministry and trust them completely! In the long run, however, you've created an unhealthy ministry culture: Far too few people doing far too much work.

It makes more sense to pile on the praise for what our volunteers are already doing instead of pressuring them to do even more. I'm the father of two children and have learned that praise almost always works better than pressure. When my daughter Kayla was struggling in math, I praised her for her effort even though she got a C on her report card. I guess I could have pressured her by challenging her commitment to the mathematic sciences, but I recognized that she was doing the best she could in that area while she juggled several other subjects.

Volunteers are juggling all kinds of stuff: their families, their careers, their life outside of church, and so on. And yet, most churches keep pressuring them to do even more. Would you be OK with a volunteer who could only commit to serving once a month? How about a volunteer who was shy around large groups but was an incredible note writer? Instead of coming up with our predetermined lists of what we think our volunteers need to do and pressuring them to fit that mold, how about letting them find their unique niche and cheering them on?!

As for the faithful, trustworthy, loyal volunteers in your ministry that have been doing so much for so long, take them to a nice lunch, praise their commitment to your ministry, and promise that you'll find others to help lighten the load.

(By the way, Kayla is now an A student in math.)

Notes and Things

Encouragement is great, but encouragement that you can keep is even better! Here are a whole bunch of fun, simple ideas your volunteers can wrap their arms around, hang on their wall, and even drink from!

23. The Name Note

Supplies Needed: poster board, construction paper, or greeting card
Cost: varies

Make an encouraging acronym using the name of your volunteer. Here are some ideas for how you can use it as an encouragement piece.

- Attach it to a greeting card.
- Draw it on a poster board, and hang it in the volunteer's office.
- Write it on a coffee mug.
- Put it on a sign on the person's front door.
- Write it on construction paper, and frame it.

Example
Kindhearted
Available
Rad small group leader
Excited about what God is doing
Nurturing spirit

24. The Napkin Note

Supplies Needed: napkin from a restaurant, black marker
Cost: free

The next time you go to lunch with a volunteer—don't forget to grab a napkin! After your lunch, take a moment to jot down a quick encouragement note or thanks to your volunteer on a restaurant napkin. If you talked about something specific, refer to it on the napkin. It's a great way to communicate that you valued your time together. You might also use the "napkin note" when you run into a volunteer and his or her family while you are out to eat. Grab a napkin, and jot a quick note. Bumping into someone is always a great reminder for encouragement, and it's nice for people to know you are thinking about them!

EXAMPLES

- *"Thanks so much for having lunch the other day! You are doing an awesome job ministering to students! Thanks for your time and energy."*

- *"Hey pal! I loved your ideas about helping students grow in their faith— especially the one about starting a new Bible study! Let's talk more...I would love to hear more of your insight. Thanks for having lunch. You are awesome!"*

25. BROWN BAG IT

SUPPLIES NEEDED: brown paper lunch sack, note card, lunch gift certificate (optional)
COST: free (or under $10 per person)

A creative way to invite a volunteer to lunch is to send that person a brown paper lunch sack with the time, date, and place written on the bag. You can drop a quick note, an uplifting Scripture, or a reminder inside the bag for a little added encouragement. You can also use lunch sacks to invite a group of volunteers to lunch by making it a contest. The first one to get there with his or her lunch sack gets a free lunch.

The brown bag can also serve as a little encouragement gift instead of an invitation. Stick a gift certificate to a volunteer's favorite lunch spot inside with a note attached, "Have lunch on us today! You mean so much to our ministry!" Mail it, deliver it to work, deliver it to school, or have a student deliver it.

TOP 5 SIGNS THAT SOMEONE MAY NOT MAKE A GOOD YOUTH MINISTRY VOLUNTEER

5. He has an "I HATE YOU!" tattoo on his forearm.

4. He thinks *fun* is actually a four-letter word.

3. Her idea of relevant music is Barney sing-a-long songs.

2. He thinks flannel boards may be the next big thing.

1. She's heard of teenagers but has never actually seen one.

26. Special Delivery

Supplies Needed: a yummy snack; a plate, wrapper, or other container

Cost: under $5 per person

Around 3 p.m. most people start getting a little restless at work. Show up at your volunteer's workplace with a milkshake, a smoothie, a huge candy bar, or a plate of chocolate chip cookies. Write a quick note of encouragement on the cup, wrapper, or plate, and leave it at the front desk. Or deliver it right to your friend! It's a guaranteed midday revival. Your leaders will love it!

27. RANDOM POSTCARDS

SUPPLIES NEEDED: postcard, postage
COST: under $1 per person

Postcards are everywhere! Pick up a variety of goofy postcards to send to your volunteers. You can find them at a gift shop, the grocery store, or a gas station, or pick some up when you are traveling. It doesn't matter where they are from; in fact, the stranger they are the better! Postcards are also easy to keep in your car, your office, your backpack, or your briefcase. The next time you have to wait at the dentist office or to pick up your kids from school, use that time to write postcards. It's an easy encouragement tool that you can always keep handy.

EXAMPLE

Find a postcard with a really peaceful scene on it, such as a peaceful lake, a sunset, or a quiet beach. Start the postcard with Psalm 62:5-6: "Find rest, O my soul, in God alone; my hope comes from him. He alone is my rock and my salvation; he is my fortress, I will not be shaken." Finish the postcard with an encouraging note, "I hope you find rest in the Lord today. Take time out to meet with him. Rest, rest, rest in him! Have a great week!"

TIP
Enlist the help of friends and family to find postcards. If you know people who are traveling, have them pick up a few for you!

28. PLANTING SEEDS

SUPPLIES NEEDED: packet of seeds, sticky label or note card
COST: under $1 per person

Packets of flower or vegetable seeds are typically inexpensive. Pick up a packet of seeds, and attach a note to your volunteer, thanking that person for planting spiritual seeds in the lives of others. It's a great way to remind your volunteers that, even though they don't always see the harvest or the fruit, God is using the seeds they are planting.

EXAMPLE

"You are doing an amazing job with the students in your ministry! Thanks for planting the seeds of Christ in their hearts each week. They are being impacted by you daily! Even if you don't see the fruit right away, keep gardening!"

TIP

If you know your volunteer has a favorite flower or plant, try to find those seeds. It's not only a great encouragement but a great gift as well! If you want to make this a more guy-friendly idea, try sunflower seeds. They make great snacks!

29. THANK-YOU BOOK

SUPPLIES NEEDED: small spiral notebook of blank paper, pictures of volunteer with students
COST: under $5 per person

Find a small spiral notebook or a small pad of paper, and make a little booklet full of thank-yous for your volunteer. Write a different thank-you statement on every page. If you have any photos of your volunteers in action, be sure to add those into the booklet. You can also add student notes, Scripture, parent notes, stories, or funny quotes. It will become a very fond ministry memory for your friend.

EXAMPLES

- *"Thank you for listening!"*
- *"Thank you for going without sleep at camp!"*
- *"Thank you for seeing the potential in students!"*
- *"Thanks for being part of the team!"*

TIP

You can make the booklets generic and "mass-produce" them, or you can make a custom one for each volunteer. The custom booklet definitely makes a huge impact on a volunteer's life.

30. Cut It Out

Supplies Needed: daily newspaper or magazine, postage, envelope
Cost: under $1 per person

TIP

Keep a file on hand in your office, and begin saving stuff as you read. You will be surprised at how much stuff you can collect and send out to volunteers!

As you read the newspaper or your favorite magazine, skim the pages for funny pictures, comics, quotes, or statements. When you come across something unique, cut it out and send it to a volunteer. Write a quick note along the bottom of the picture like "Have a great day," "This made me think of you," or "Hope your day goes better than this!"

31. Picture This

Supplies Needed: pictures from camp, small frame
Cost: under $5 per person

Take pictures of your volunteers with students. Whether it's a small group Bible study or a summer camp cabin, take pictures! Any pictures you take can serve as a postcard for an encouragement note. Not only is it a cool postcard, but it also gives volunteers a great picture of their ministry in action. It's a memory, an inspiration, and a reminder of what God is doing

TEAM TALK

"Getting a framed picture of my group of guys at camp was great! With all the good times we shared, it's a nice reminder of why I participated as a counselor and it gets me pumped up to do it again next year."

—Gerry Rojas
Single adult; weekend volunteer;
camp counselor extraordinaire

through them. If you want to go a step further, put it in a frame and have the frame engraved with, "Thanks for serving the Lord by serving students." Your volunteer will keep it forever. Hand it out at a trip reunion, or send it to your friend in the mail!

TIP

Instead of using just one picture, create a collage of photos from the trip and put it in a frame.

32. COPYCAT

SUPPLIES NEEDED: envelope, postage
COST: under $1 per person

Go to your nearest photocopy machine, and copy your hand making the number five. Write at the top of the copy, "The Top 5 Reasons You Are an Awesome Minister." Above each finger on the copy, jot some words of encouragement and thanks. Write a couple of funny things and a couple of serious things, then mail it off to the person you want to encourage. This is a great one if you don't have a lot of time!

EXAMPLE

5. You don't charge us to use your minivan for events.
4. Students love you.
3. You have an awesome passion for ministry.
2. You love to eat pizza.
1. You have a huge servant's heart.

33. Make-Believe Mad Libs

Supplies Needed: none
Cost: free

Create your own version of the classic "Mad Lib." Write a mad lib that includes clever things about your specific ministry. Then, fill in the blanks in your own handwriting with nouns, verbs, adverbs, and adjectives to give it a personal touch. Fill it in with funny and serious words. Obviously, the finished product will make little or no sense, but if you add a few accurate pieces of information, it can create a memorable note. This takes some thought and time, but it's well worth it.

Example

Once upon a time in our youth group, there was a lady

named _MAGGIE_ **who went to** _DISNEYLAND_ **with the**
[PROPER NOUN]   [PLACE]

eighth graders. While there, she ate _SPINACH_ **and**
[FOOD]

CAKE **and even drank some** _GRAVY_ . **She also helped**
[FOOD]   [LIQUID]

lead a _FUNKY_ **small group each week and was always**
[ADJECTIVE]

quick to _JOG_ **whenever someone asked. Because of**
[VERB]

her, our ministry has never been the same.

34. Overachiever Award

Supplies Needed: varies
Cost: varies

Do you have those volunteers who always seem to go above and beyond the call of duty? Has someone gone the extra mile? Do you have volunteers who constantly overachieve and do more than you expect? Unfortunately, these efforts often go unnoticed and unrecognized! Take a moment in a volunteer meeting, a team dinner, or youth group meeting to recognize one of those volunteers as your ministry's overachiever!

The "Overachiever Award" is your chance to get those creative juices flowing. You can make an Overachiever Award out of just about anything. Over the years in our youth ministry, we have used everything from a toy airplane to a pineapple to recognize a volunteer's efforts. There are many different options with the Overachiever Award, and we've included a few ideas for you. But the best way to do this is to use your own creativity to customize a special award for one of your overachieving volunteers!

FUN OVERACHIEVER IDEAS

- Trophies—Even adults are proud to bring home a trophy! Go to a local trophy shop, and find a small trophy that might best represent your volunteer. Have the shop engrave the volunteer's name, the date the person will receive the award, and a small phrase highlighting the great work he or she has done. We have a lady named Remy on our volunteer team who is an awesome encourager. When we decided to give her the Overachiever Award, we determined that the best way to recognize her was to give her a trophy with a cheerleader on top. The trophy read: Remy—November 2003—Thanks for being our Cheerleader!

> **TIP**
> Shop around at garage sales for old trophies. Or have members of your church donate old trophies to your youth ministry. It is very inexpensive to have a little nameplate engraved at the trophy shop.

EXAMPLES

- *Matt Hall, football trophy: "Thanks for being a team player!"*
- *Ron Edwards, baseball trophy: "You've hit a home run with students!"*

- Plaques—Plaques are also available at your local trophy shop. The cool thing about a plaque is that you can customize it by putting a photo inside. Find a photo of your overachiever volunteer with students or doing the ministry he or she is being recognized for. This will become a nice keepsake for your volunteer.

> **TIP**
> This also works well with a generic plastic frame, available at almost all discount stores. Grab a permanent marker and a picture of your overachiever in action and you're all set!

- Certificates—This is an "oldie but goody." There are many creative ways to use a simple certificate to honor an overachiever. Certificates can be funny or serious. You can customize them for individual volunteers, and they are very inexpensive so you can do several at one time. For example, we were honoring all of our junior high ministry small group leaders at an appreciation dinner, and each volunteer received a certificate. Each overachiever certificate was created especially for each volunteer.

EXAMPLES

- *Kathy Dodd received the "Guest Relations" award. She was amazing at greeting and welcoming students.*
- *Karolyn Thompson received the "Martha Stewart" award. She had the incredible gift of hospitality.*
- *Rich Kelly received the "MVP" award. He was a team player who helped out in many different ministry areas.*

- **Random Objects**—With this type of award, you will need to think of simple but fun objects to award your volunteers. For example, we had some leaders at summer camp that went above and beyond. We spray painted toy airplanes gold and wrote "Above and Beyond the Call of Duty" on the side. It was just a simple way to show them that we recognized they were awesome, but it was not your average award. (If your meeting has a theme, this award works great!)

EXAMPLES
- *hammer: "Thanks for using the tools God gave you!"*
- *potted plant: "Thanks for planting seeds!"*
- *pineapple: "Thanks for being fruitful!"*

TEAM TALK

"In the ten years that I've been working in our youth ministry, I have been blessed to receive the Overachiever Award three times. For some reason, it never gets old! It means so much to know that the paid staff notices when volunteers go the extra mile. For me personally, the Overachiever Award gave me the confidence to continue doing God's work within the ministry that he has called me to serve."

–Rich Kelly
School teacher; ten-year volunteer; extremely bald

MORE THAN A MEETING

When you have volunteers, it's inevitable that you are going to meet. So, why not make it "more than a meeting"? Put a little creativity into your regular meeting time. Not only will they have fun, but volunteers will also walk away feeling encouraged and cared for. On the following pages, you'll find some sample ideas for meeting elements to help make your next gathering more than a meeting.

TEAM MEETING ELEMENTS

- **Create a theme.** A theme is a great way to plan a meeting with your volunteers. It helps set the tone for your time together, and it gives a cool feeling to your meeting. It also communicates time and effort on your part, which translates into encouragement and care to your volunteers.

- **Decorate.** Take a few moments before your volunteer meeting to decorate the meeting room to match your theme. Decorating adds an extra "wow!" to the experience.

- **Enjoy a meal together.** Everyone loves food! Why not add food as an element to your next volunteer meeting? It's also great to sit around a table together enjoying dinner and casual conversation; the dinner table is a great place to share life with your volunteers.

- **Provide training.** When you're in the trenches of youth ministry, you need training. Whether you're a rookie or a seasoned veteran, ongoing ministry training is a necessity. Take time to train your volunteers. Even seasoned veterans need new ideas. Everyone can benefit from simple reminders and new tricks of the trade.

  Here are just a few training topics you might want to cover:
    —"The Values of Your Ministry"
    —"The Purpose and Vision of Your Ministry"
    —"How to Discipline in Love"
    —"How to Lead Someone Into a Relationship With Christ"
    —"How to Be a Better Listener"

- **Facilitate connections among volunteers.** Whether you have two volunteers or twenty-two volunteers, get them connected with one another. Each volunteer has something unique to contribute to your ministry. Get them talking with one another, spending time together, and sharing life and ministry experiences. Volunteers will feel very encouraged by hearing stories from other volunteers who are in the trenches.

- **Include games, giveaways, and fun.** Laughter, fun, and free stuff are always good elements in a volunteer meeting. Play your favorite youth ministry games, create a "themed" game, or do a huge raffle or giveaway. It's a simple way to have a great time together, laugh a little, and lift spirits.

- **Spend time in worship.** A great way to make a meeting more than a meeting is to provide an opportunity for praise and worship. Volunteers often miss out on the adult corporate worship times due to their commitment to ministry. Start the meeting or wrap it up with a short time of worship.

- **Share faith stories.** A great way to encourage your volunteers is to let them hear from other volunteers who are on the same path. It's awesome to hear people share their stories of what God is doing in their heart and in their ministry. Find volunteers or students to share about their personal faith journey.

- **Invite a guest speaker.** Bring in a guest speaker to encourage your volunteers. They probably love to be encouraged by you, but why not bring in an outside source to "love on" your leaders? For example, ask your senior pastor or your worship pastor to share a devotion. Or bring in a youth pastor from another church or a visiting missionary to share with your team.

- **Screen a video.** Show a funny or inspirational video clip. Partner the clip with training, a Bible study, or a ministry pep talk. Or show one just for fun to make your volunteers laugh!

- **Lead a Bible study.** Most meetings start with prayer, but why not start it out with a short Bible study that relates to the theme or training time? Ask one of the volunteers to prepare a ten-minute lesson and share it with the team.

- **Go on a "field trip."** At your next meeting, try surprising your volunteer leaders by taking them on a field trip.

When they arrive, have a couple of cars waiting to take them bowling, out for ice cream, or to a cool restaurant. You may want to take them somewhere that relates to the theme of the night. For example, if your theme is "Let's Go to the Movies," have cars waiting to take them to a new release.

- **Commission them.** When new volunteers join your ministry team, commission them for ministry. Take time in your next meeting to gather around them and pray for their work with students.

- **"You saw it here first!"** Introduce new vision and direction to your volunteers before anyone else hears it or sees it. It's encouraging to them to know that their opinion is valued. Let them be a part of the vision-casting process in your youth ministry.

- **Give awards.** Take a few moments in your volunteer meetings to highlight volunteers who have gone the extra mile. Recognize the big things and the little things. We give away several overachiever awards as a traditional part of every team meeting.

CREATIVE MEETING THEMES

Each meeting theme suggested on the following pages includes some of the elements we just outlined. You don't need to do everything listed to have a successful meeting. These are just ideas to get you started!

35. BACK TO SCHOOL

This is a great theme for the beginning of the school year.

DECORATIONS
- metal lunch box in the center of the table surrounded by rulers, pencils, crayons, chalk
- chalkboards, construction paper
- old school pictures of kids and teachers
- finger paintings hanging on the wall

FOOD
- homemade sandwiches wrapped in wax paper or in a sandwich bag (peanut butter and jelly, turkey, tuna)
- apples and bananas
- individually wrapped cookies, chips, fruit snacks, string cheese
- small milk cartons, juice boxes, sodas

TRAINING TOPICS
- "Remember When?" (Have volunteers share what life was like when they were students.)
- "How to Be a Better Teacher" (Share insights about effective Bible teaching.)

VOLUNTEER CONNECTION QUESTIONS
- What was your first day of junior high or high school like?
- What are you looking forward to this school year?
- What are your ministry goals for the year?
- What are some good ideas for supporting students as they go back to school?

GAME IDEA
- Have each of your volunteers send you a school picture from any grade. Put them together on one sheet of paper, and create a Who's Who game for your volunteers.

COMMISSIONING

- Chances are if you are kicking off a new year, you will have some new volunteers ministering with you. Take a moment to recognize them and pray for them. You could do this every time you have a new volunteer, or you could do it once or twice a year with groups of volunteers.
- Have your current volunteers gather around each new volunteer and pray for their ministry.

EXTRAS

- Stuff backpacks with inexpensive goodies—candy, soda, school supplies, a gift certificate—for all of your volunteers.

36. FALL KICKOFF (FOOTBALL THEME)

DECORATIONS

- football helmets, footballs
- pompoms, team jerseys
- green turf
- referee whistle
- football gear (Ask your local recreation center if they can let you borrow some.)

FOOD

- big sub sandwiches
- nachos, buffalo wings
- sodas, sports drinks

TRAINING TOPICS

- "Reach for the Goal!"
- "Tackling Discipline" (or another ministry topic such as "Tackling Safety" or "Tackling Small Groups")

VOLUNTEER CONNECTION QUESTIONS

- What is your favorite sport?
- If you could be any athlete in history, who would you be and why?
- What makes a true champion?

GAME IDEAS

- football trivia
- football toss—Create a target or a bull's-eye, and have volunteer QBs aim for the center.

GIVEAWAYS

- Get tickets to a local college or professional football team game. Give them away as a door prize or a raffle prize. (Or get enough tickets so that everyone can go! Another fun team event would be to attend a local high school football game together.)
- Get a water bottle for each volunteer in your ministry. Put your ministry name on it or a fun encouragement note saying, "You can do it!" or "Thanks for being part of the team!"

GUEST SPEAKERS

- If it's possible, bring in a professional athlete to do a short devotion.
- Have a volunteer who played sports give a short devotion.

ABSOLUTELY NOTHING

It's quite possible that the best way to encourage and energize your team of volunteers is by doing absolutely nothing! As a leader, you need to be on the lookout for those volunteers in your ministry who are too busy and give them permission to take an "absolutely nothing" break. During their week or two of absolutely nothing, promise them that they will hear absolutely nothing from you or your ministry. Far too many ministry leaders take advantage of and encourage those who are willing to volunteer long hours. Their role in your ministry is important, but let's face it, it's not as important as some of the other roles they play. Volunteers are also parents, spouses, friends, employees, bosses, and so much more. They are doing their best to juggle all the stuff that's important to them and will eventually begin to drop stuff. Don't let that happen! Give them permission to take time off to refocus, to slow down, to mow their lawn, and to quit "juggling" for just a little while. Volunteers do a lot. They teach Sunday school, they clean classrooms, they lead fund-raisers, they call parents, and they organize activities. Tell them thanks by asking them to do absolutely nothing!

TIP

At an upcoming meeting or gathering, talk to your volunteer team about the "Absolutely Nothing" concept. When you're finished, have a drawing and award the winner a coupon good for "Absolutely Nothing!" Tell them that they should all be prepared to get their own coupon in the mail sometime in the next several months.

37. WESTERN

DECORATIONS
- red and white checkered tablecloths
- cowboy hats, bandanas, cowboy boots
- Mason jars filled with wild flowers, bales of hay
- an old western movie playing on a TV in the room
- country music playing
- western costumes

FOOD
- barbecued beef sandwiches, ribs, chicken
- baked beans, corn on the cob, watermelon, corn bread

TRAINING TOPICS
- "How to Lasso a Kid in the Community"
- "Wrangling Up New Leaders"

GAME IDEAS
- Play a game of horseshoes.
- Bob for apples. Attach a number on an apple that goes with a gift certificate or a prize.

AWARDS
- Get rodeo trophies engraved for your volunteers.

38. LUAU

DECORATIONS
- Tiki torches (for outdoors)
- fishbowls in the center of the tables
- Hawaiian-print fabric, Hawaiian music playing
- Create coconut votives by cutting the coconut in half and placing a votive candle inside.
- pineapples, grass skirts, Hawaiian shirts

VOLUNTEER CONNECTION QUESTIONS
- Where is your favorite place to relax?
- Where would you take your dream vacation?
- Where is your favorite place to meet with the Lord each day?
- What is an area of your life in which you need to find rest in God?

WORSHIP
- Grab an acoustic guitar and enjoy worship together as a team.

FAITH STORY
- Have one of your volunteers share his or her personal faith story.

BIBLE STUDY TOPICS
- "Rest and Relaxation in God's Word"
- "Ministering From a 'Full Well' "

FIELD TRIP
- Take a trip to get "shaved ice" or tropical ice cream somewhere.

EXTRAS
- Give each volunteer a flower lei upon arrival.
- Have everyone come dressed for a luau.
- Find someone to come and give hula dance instructions to your volunteer team.
- *Mahalo* means "thank you" in Hawaiian. To make thank-you notes for your volunteers, find Hawaiian-looking floral stationery and write *Mahalo!* on the inside.

39. BREAKFAST BASH

DECORATIONS
- cozy blankets
- pillows
- beanbags
- cartoons playing on a TV

FOOD
- pancakes, waffles, French toast
- cold cereal and milk
- bagels, toast, toaster pastries
- muffins, doughnuts

GAME IDEAS
- Saturday morning cartoon trivia—Create a cartoon trivia game that spans all decades.
- breakfast cereal character trivia—Put pictures of ten different breakfast cereal "mascots" on a sheet of paper, and have volunteers try to guess who's who.

WORSHIP

- Take a morning "Prayer Walk." *This is a cool activity for your volunteers to do together and a great way to get them interacting during a meeting.*
- Pray as a volunteer team for your ministry.
- Create prayer stations for your team to rotate through.
- Walk through your youth room or your church campus, and pray for students who are going to come through your doors.
- Walk through your local community, and pray for areas where students hang out.

FIELD TRIP

- Have your meeting at a local doughnut shop. Ask the manager if you could have exclusive use of the shop after hours for one evening.

EXTRAS

- Have people come dressed in their pajamas.
- Give everyone a half-dozen doughnuts to take home.
- Give out mini boxes of Frosted Flakes with a note attached saying "You're GR-R-REAT!"

40. LET'S GO TO THE MOVIES

DECORATIONS

- red carpet with rope lights
- big popcorn buckets on the table filled with popcorn
- strips of film on the table
- tickets
- movie posters
- Hollywood sign, director's chair
- Have a classic movie playing while volunteers are arriving.

FOOD

- buttered popcorn, hot dogs
- nachos and pretzels
- boxes of candy
- sodas

TRAINING TOPICS

- "You Don't Have to Be a Star to Be Used by God."
- "God Has an Incredible Script for Every Life."

VOLUNTEER CONNECTION QUESTIONS
- What is your favorite movie theater snack?
- Who is your favorite movie star?
- If you had an opportunity to share Christ's love with that person, how would you do it?
- Can you think of a student you could share Jesus with in the same way?

BIBLE STUDY
- Find a powerful movie clip, and talk about its significance. Find a Scripture that will accompany the clip.

EXTRAS
- Have a screening of a classic movie after the meeting is over.
- Give away individual packages of microwave popcorn with a note attached reading, "You are amazing! Each of these pieces of popcorn represents a thank-you!"
- "You Saw It Here First!"—Give volunteers a "sneak preview" of upcoming events or the launch of a new program or idea.

41. THANK YOU

DECORATIONS
- Create a "family" dinner table.
- Place fall leaves, pumpkins, and cornucopias in the center of the table.
- Create pumpkin votives by carving out the center of the pumpkin and placing a votive candle inside.

FOOD
- Create a traditional Thanksgiving dinner.
- Have a potluck, and have everyone bring a dish to share.
- Enlist parents in your ministry to help bring food.

VOLUNTEER CONNECTION QUESTIONS
- What are you most thankful for?
- What student do you want to thank God for? Why?
- What do you need prayer for in your life and in your ministry?

WORSHIP
- Spend time worshipping in song together.
- Spend time praising God in words and prayer together.

GUEST SPEAKER

- Have someone from your church family or someone on your church staff come and give a special "thank-you" to your team. It would be great to get your senior pastor or an elder in your church to come and speak. The speaker could also do a video message if he or she is unable to make it to the meeting.

EXTRAS

- Have students in your ministry write a "thank-you" note to each volunteer, and use the notes as place cards at the table.
- Create an original worship CD for each volunteer in your ministry as a thank-you gift.

TOP 5
"ONE WORD" ENCOURAGEMENTS

5. Awesome!

4. Yes.

3. Thanks.

2. Wow!

1. Youareincrediblethanksforallthewaysyouserveourministry!

42. LOVE

DECORATIONS
- Decorate for a Valentine's party.
- hearts, red tablecloths
- candles
- flowers in the center of tables
- Cupids

FOOD
- all desserts!
- chocolate-dipped strawberries
- cheesecake, chocolate cake
- ice cream sundaes
- fudge, homemade candy
- heart candies

TRAINING TOPICS
- "How to Love Students Unconditionally"
- "How to Talk to a Student Who Is in Love"

GUEST SPEAKER
- Have a married couple in your ministry or your church come and share about their story—how they met, what God means to their relationship, and so on.

BIBLE STUDY TOPICS
- "The Second Greatest Commandment" (See Matthew 22:38-39.)
- "A Loving Reminder" (See John 3:16.)
- "Love Is the Greatest." (See 1 Corinthians 13:13.)

GATHERINGS OR GET-TOGETHERS

Not every meeting or gathering with your volunteers needs to have a formal agenda. Encouraging meetings come in all different forms. Invite families, have fun together, play as a team; your volunteers will feel encouraged when you love on their families and when you spend time with them.

43. OLD-FASHIONED FAMILY PICNIC

- Eat potluck style.
- Sit around long tables.
- Do a potato sack race and bob for apples.
- Hold a cakewalk and a pie-eating contest.
- Award blue ribbons to game winners.
- Play a softball game.

44. TAILGATE PARTY

- Meet in an empty parking lot.
- Park all cars in a circle with tailgates down.
- Barbecue hamburgers and hot dogs.
- Tune in radios to a sports channel.
- Have people wear their favorite jersey.
- Bring out portable basketball hoops.

45. FIESTA

- Make your own tacos and burritos.
- Have mariachi music playing.
- Fill piñatas with candy for the kids.
- Fill a piñata for the adults.
- Decorate with bright colors, sombreros, and blankets.

TEAM TALK

"Serving God in our junior high ministry is one of the greatest experiences I have ever had. The bottom line is, it's not just about the kids, but it's the entire package that makes this an incredible experience. Knowing I'm prayed for each week—that I'm equipped and encouraged—has enabled me to literally become a small group *pastor* to ten junior high guys each week and in turn impact their lives for Christ. Kurt is not just the junior high pastor but he's also a great friend...I can't imagine trying to do ministry without the support I've received."

—Dan Gutwein
Husband, father; small group leader; ministry cheerleader

SHARING LIFE

We have a great tradition in our junior high ministry. Each year at our Christmas party, we give Bibles to those celebrating a five-year anniversary as a volunteer in our ministry and a watch to those celebrating ten years. When we first came up with the idea, we figured that we could easily afford the cost of the gifts because, after all, how many people are really going to stick around that long? Last Christmas we gave away five Bibles and three watches. That's eight people who have combined for fifty-five years worth of ministry to our students! Gary Eilts, a volunteer who helps us design our weekend program, has been on our team for *fifteen* years!

Volunteers join our team because they have a heart for students and want to use their gifts to make a difference. They stay on our team for the long haul because we don't just share ministry, we share *life*. For most of our volunteers, the junior high ministry team has become their own "church" within the church. We bring each other meals when there's a sickness or new birth, we baby-sit for each other, and we show up to help when one of us is painting the kitchen.

It's great to have a lot of volunteers playing a variety of roles in our ministry; we couldn't be effective without them. It's even better to have a lot of people playing a variety of roles in our ministry who are also sharing life's journey together.

MEETING PERSONAL NEEDS

Believe it or not, your volunteers actually have a life outside the church and your ministry! One of the biggest mistakes a leader can make is to seem un-interested in or unaware of the daily lives of those they are leading. Over the years, we've missed a few crucial opportunities to encourage and support volunteers in their time of need. Hopefully these ideas will keep you from making that same mistake.

A NEW BABY

46. NEW ARRIVAL BASKET

SUPPLIES NEEDED: large basket, baby items
COST: under $20 per person

Buy a large basket, and have other volunteers, parents, and students contribute items for it. It's a great way to meet some "new parent" needs and to show that your ministry wants to celebrate this special addition in their life.

Ideas for basket contents:
- rattle and other baby toys
- a card from your ministry
- baby socks, baby utensils, package of diapers, wipes
- baby brush and comb, baby lullaby CD, soft stuffed animal

47. BABY SHOWER

SUPPLIES NEEDED: invitations, decorations, party favors, dessert and drinks, poster board

COST: varies

Open up the youth room for a baby shower! If you have more than one new arrival in your ministry, throw a group shower for your new babies! Again, involve parents, students, and other volunteers. Have a potluck or a barbecue, and have everyone bring something. Think of some fun youth ministry games that you could turn into baby shower games, and have everyone chip in for a group gift. Encourage students to decorate, and invite parents to write words of wisdom on poster board and hang it on the wall.

48. MEAL DELIVERY

SUPPLIES NEEDED: none

COST: free

As a treat for your volunteer, set up a meal rotation for a couple of weeks after the baby is born. Involve parents, students, and other volunteers who would each like to sign up to bring dinner one evening. Check with the new parents before arranging this. Ask about what foods they like and if they have any allergies. This is an awesome way to show care and support in the beginning of a crazy season of life!

49. BABY-SITTING

SUPPLIES NEEDED: none

COST: free

Some volunteers might be on baby number two or three. In that case, set up some baby-sitting for the other children. Have someone take out the other kids for ice cream or a movie. It's not only great for your volunteer, but it also gives you an opportunity to minister to their kids and make them feel special. You can also set up baby-sitting on an ongoing basis. For example, set up a schedule for students to baby-sit every Friday for two months.

50. Maid for a Month

Supplies Needed: none
Cost: free

If you're able to set this up, it will be the ultimate new parent gift! Find someone to be a "Maid for a Month" for your volunteer. Have the "maid" come in once a week for a month to clean house, do laundry, make beds, and so on. It's not easy to find such a person, but it's a wonderful way to minister to your volunteer.

TIP

Call around to housecleaning services listed in the phone book, and ask if they are willing to donate services or give you a discounted service. It never hurts to ask, and you might end up with someone who is excited to help out!

Engagements, Weddings, or Anniversaries

51. How Many Cards?

Supplies Needed: greeting cards, postage
Cost: varies

Buy and write anniversary greetings in multiple cards; you'll want one card for each year your volunteer has been married. Get separate postage for each card, and drop them all in the mail. (Or if you prefer, send multiple e-mail cards.) You can do this on your own, or you can enlist other volunteers to participate. Try to coordinate it so the special volunteer receives all of the cards on the anniversary date. For extra encouragement, include a small gift with each card.

Examples
- *twenty cards for twenty years*
- *fifteen roses and fifteen cards for fifteen years*
- *ten fresh-baked muffins and ten cards for ten years*
- *one chocolate cake and one card for one year*

52. Date Night Surprise

Supplies Needed: a basket, date night items
Cost: under $15 per person

Create an anniversary "date night basket." Fill it up with little items to help the special couple celebrate their anniversary day.

Ideas for basket contents:
• homemade anniversary card
• favorite two-liter bottle of soda
• dessert for two
• favorite candy
• movie rental coupon
• candles

53. Students Need to Know!

Supplies Needed: none
Cost: free

Acknowledge your married couples in front of students. When they hit an anniversary milestone, celebrate it with students! Make a big deal about it! Students need to see God-honoring marriages in action. They need to see people celebrating love and commitment. At your weekly meeting with students, bring the couple to the front, praise them for their journey, and pray for their future. You can also do this with couples who are about to get married. Have them share their journey of engagement and then, as a group, pray for their marriage.

54. Showered With Love

Supplies Needed: invitations, decorations, party favors, food and drinks
Cost: varies

Throw a wedding shower for your engaged volunteers. Create a fun theme like "Things you didn't register for, but you really need"—earplugs for snoring, smoke alarm for cooking, stamps for thank-you notes, condiments for the fridge, and an advice jar with little tidbits from your married volunteers. Invite your other volunteers and their families to join the party.

55. FAMILY DONATION
SUPPLIES NEEDED: none
COST: free

It's expensive for couples to get away! Help provide something special for them by finding a family in the church to donate the use of an RV, a summer home, a nice car, or a time share. Time alone together is a huge gift and a wonderful encouragement for married couples.

ROUGH SEASONS

56. "THINKING OF YOU" VOICE MAIL
SUPPLIES NEEDED: none
COST: free

When you know a volunteer is going through a tough time, take a moment to call that person when you know he or she won't be at home. Leave a message of encouragement on your friend's voice mail. Read a comforting Scripture, such as Romans 5:1-5: "Therefore, since we have been justified through faith, we have peace with God through our Lord Jesus Christ, through whom we have gained access by faith into this grace in which we now stand. And we rejoice in the hope of the glory of God. Not only so, but we also rejoice in our sufferings, because we know that suffering produces perseverance; perseverance, character; and character, hope. And hope does not disappoint us, because God has poured out his love into our hearts by the Holy Spirit, whom he has given us."

57. TALK IT OUT

SUPPLIES NEEDED: none
COST: varies

As your volunteers go through rough seasons, other volunteers on your team might want to help out in the encouragement effort. If you know of people who want to help, coordinate a group contribution to pay for counseling sessions. Many volunteers go through things that your team might not be equipped to handle. Professional counseling might be just what your volunteer needs to make it through a tough time.

58. E-MAIL LOVE

SUPPLIES NEEDED: none
COST: free

Tough times come in all different sizes, shapes, and forms. You might have volunteers who are out of work, going through financial difficulties, or facing challenges with one of their children. Chances are, you come in contact with someone *every week* who is in need of encouragement. Send an e-mail once a day for a week with an encouraging note and a Scripture passage to those friends who are hurting.

EXAMPLE

"Just wanted to let you know that I am thinking of you today. I will be praying for you as you deal with finding a new job. Psalm 33:11 says, 'But the plans of the Lord stand firm forever, the purposes of his heart through all generations.' Remember that God is in control and he has a plan."

TIP

Here are some other Scripture passages you could use in this situation.

- Jeremiah 29:11—"'For I know the plans I have for you,' declares the Lord, 'plans to prosper you and not to harm you, plans to give you hope and a future.'"
- Matthew 5:3-10—"Blessed are the poor in spirit, for theirs is the kingdom of heaven. Blessed are those who mourn, for they will be comforted. Blessed are the meek, for they will inherit the earth. Blessed are those who hunger and thirst for righteousness, for they will be filled. Blessed are the merciful, for they will be shown mercy. Blessed are the pure in heart, for they will see God. Blessed are the peacemakers, for they will be called sons of God. Blessed are those who are persecuted because of righteousness, for theirs is the kingdom of heaven."
- John 15:4a—"Remain in me, and I will remain in you."
- 2 Corinthians 1:3-4—"Praise be to the God and Father of our Lord Jesus Christ, the Father of compassion and the God of all comfort, who comforts us in all our troubles, so that we can comfort those in any trouble with the comfort we ourselves have received from God."

59. NOTE BOUQUET

SUPPLIES NEEDED: small vase, floral sticks, note cards, ribbon, silk flowers
COST: under $15 per person

Flowers are beautiful, but they don't last very long. They certainly don't last long enough to provide comfort through several hard weeks or months in a person's life. Instead of giving a bouquet of flowers, give a bouquet of encouragement notes! Have parents, students, and fellow volunteers each write a note of encouragement including a Scripture passage they turn to when they go through rough seasons. Put each note on a floral stick, and arrange them in a vase. Design the vase and note cards to look like a beautiful floral arrangement. Add in some silk flowers, and wrap the vase in ribbon or raffia. Then, make a special delivery to your volunteer who is hurting. It's a gift of encouragement that can provide hope day after day.

TOP 5 THINGS YOUR VOLUNTEERS WILL RARELY HEAR A STUDENT SAY

5. "Can you please teach just a little longer?"

4. "This time, it actually *was* me."

3. "I'd like to stay late and help you clean up."

2. "Can my mom sing a solo in front of the youth group?"

1. "Thanks."

ON THE ROAD...AGAIN

Traveling with students can be a unique, rewarding, and often exhausting experience. To make a trip happen, you typically need leaders. Trips, retreats, camps, and getaways are an awesome opportunity to encourage your volunteers, especially since they are pouring into students twenty-four hours a day for the length of the trip. They need it!

60. LIVING WATER

SUPPLIES NEEDED: water bottle, sticky label
COST: under $2 per person

This is a quick and easy way to encourage and inspire your leaders on a trip. Ministering to students on a trip is often a draining process. Take a moment during your week away, and revive them with a little reminder from Jesus. Replace the labels on water bottles with labels of your own. Use Scripture or a hand-written note on each label to encourage your volunteers.

TEAM TALK

"The living water bottle is great! Everyone knew they were just water bottles, but what made them so special was the extra effort—the reminder on the label that God was present to refresh us. I actually turned around and used the bottle idea with my small group of girls. It went over wonderfully. The best part was that they were so simple. Encouragement doesn't have to be hard or complicated, and this is a perfect example."

–Brittany Sanden
College student; homecoming queen; servant; loves water

Living Water
"But whoever drinks the water I give him will never thirst. Indeed, the water I give him will become in him a spring of water welling up to eternal life" John 4:14).

61. SAY CHEESE!

SUPPLIES NEEDED: camera, film
COST: varies

While you are away at camp, take a group picture of each cabin or small group together. As leaders arrive back home from camp, give it to them with a note of thanks on the back. It's a great memory as well as an encouragement for their ministry. You can have all of the students in their cabin sign the back of the picture with a note of thanks!

Thanks for everything.
See you next year, —Dawn, Bob, Luke, Stacy

62. SURVIVAL KIT

SUPPLIES NEEDED: small gift bags, note cards, kit items
COST: varies

Create a "Survival Kit" for each volunteer going on your trip. If your event has certain themes, try to incorporate things that match what you are doing. For example, our theme for camp a few years back was DRIVEN. Inside the Survival Kit, we included a toy car with a note attached.

Survival Kit ideas:
- a disposable camera
- earplugs
- aspirin
- favorite treats, chocolate
- a note of encouragement
- trip schedule and guidelines

63. STAFF STASH

SUPPLIES NEEDED: ice chest, ice, drinks, snacks
COST: varies

When you have special events for students, you always need volunteers to help make those events a success. Why not give them an extra special treat while they are serving at the event? Put together an ice chest filled with drinks and snacks that are only available to your volunteers. As they come to grab something out of the chest, take the opportunity to say "thank you" for serving at the event. (It's also a great opportunity for you to ask them to serve at the next event!)

64. VOLUNTEER OASIS

SUPPLIES NEEDED: empty cabin or space, drinks, snacks, poster board
COST: varies

This will take the idea of "Staff Stash" (Idea 63) to a whole new level! While you are away at your camp or retreat, find an empty cabin or space to create an entire area that is designated for "volunteers only." Let volunteers know that they are allowed to go to the "Volunteer Oasis" whenever they need a little break. Stock the oasis with drinks and snacks, and fill the walls with encouragement signs.

Encouragement sign ideas:
- Thanks for being here!
- You are an awesome counselor!
- Thanks for your sacrifice!
- Students' lives are being changed!

TIP

Bring some easy-to-transport furniture to set up in the "oasis," such as an inflatable couch or fold-up lawn chairs.

65. MAIL CALL

SUPPLIES NEEDED: note cards, envelopes, postage
COST: under $2 per person

A great way to encourage your leaders while they are away is to send them mail! Write letters to each of your leaders, and mail them to the camp or the retreat location. Getting mail can be an awesome surprise and encouragement for them while they are serving at camp. You can also enlist parents in this; have key parents in your ministry write notes, post-cards, or send chocolate chip cookies.

EXAMPLES
- *"Thanks so much for giving your time and energy to students this week at camp. I appreciate your taking a week off work to share Jesus with our kids. You're awesome!"*

- *"I appreciate your spending time with Abby at camp this week. It means so much to me to know that you are encouraging her and pouring into her life this week. Thank you for your impact and time."*
  —Abby's mom

66. MIDWEEK TREAT

SUPPLIES NEEDED: treat for each leader (candy, cookies, favorite soda), note cards or colored paper
COST: under $2

The halfway mark on your trip is usually the time your volunteers begin to get a little weary. Give them a refreshing treat halfway through the week. Sneak around the camp area, and leave a note and a treat on your volunteers' pillows. Do some research before the trip to find out what their favorite candy is, or give everyone the same treat with a little note attached.

> **TIP**
>
> If you have a pre-trip leaders' meeting, take a moment and find out what each leader's favorite treat is. It's a great way to pleasantly surprise people while they're away.

EXAMPLE

Give out 3 Musketeers bars and attach notes saying, "We are all in this together—one for all and all for one! You are a great part of the team this week!"

67. PRE-TRIP LEADERS' MEETING

SUPPLIES NEEDED: none
COST: free

One of the best things you can do before a trip is make sure everyone feels trained, informed, and prepared for what lies ahead. Having a pre-trip meeting with your volunteer leaders may seem unnecessary, but you'll find that it pays off. Encouragement comes in all forms! For some of your volunteers who have never been on a trip before as a counselor or leader, organization and information can be very encouraging. Helping them get to know other leaders, learning what will be expected of them on the trip, and easing the nerves before leading students for a week can really be uplifting. This meeting is a great opportunity to love on your leaders, give them your support, and encourage them before their big week away. By having a pre-trip meeting, you are communicating the importance of organization, teamwork, and planning ahead. At this meeting, they will sense your excitement and anticipation, and it will help set the tone for what's ahead. It's also a great opportunity to thank them in person for their commitment and time before the craziness of the trip actually begins.

Things to cover at your meeting:
- Print out trip expectations and responsibilities for each leader.
- Give them some tips on how to minister to students.
- Give them some tips on how to have fun with students.
- Give leaders a thank-you note before they leave for the trip.
- Give them an opportunity to ask questions.
- Try doing this meeting as a meal together!

TIP

Create a "team" notebook for each leader attending your trip. Fill the notebook with trip expectations, schedules, lists of attendees, and so on. It's a great way to encourage and equip your leaders with what they need.

TEAM TALK

"Realizing what gifts God has given you can be difficult, and we are not always confident in our own abilities. What has alleviated some of this apprehension in my ministry is having leaders who I know believe in me. When I first mentioned that the junior high needed a drama team, my leaders said, 'You're right. Go ahead and start it.' My first reaction was, 'Yeah right, I could never. I haven't even taken a drama class in my life.' But they believed in me and encouraged me to jump in and let God do the rest. Knowing that the staff has faith in me and what God can do through me has allowed me to foster my gifts and has made serving in junior high ministry all the more rewarding."

—Alanna Pearson
Young adult; four-year veteran; drama queen

68. DITCH-A-MEAL

SUPPLIES NEEDED: note cards
COST: varies

Have your leaders meet in a special spot for a "leaders only" meal (while students eat in the cafeteria). Send each leader a special note with instructions to meet at a specific location. Once leaders arrive, the possibilities are endless!

TIP

You may want to host several Ditch-a-Meals throughout the week and invite adults in smaller groups so all the leaders aren't gone at the same time. Otherwise your Ditch-a-Meal may become "Ditch-a-Meal and then go clean up the food fight in the cafeteria."

EXAMPLES

- *Call out for pizza.*
- *Have the camp staff prepare a special meal.*
- *Have food brought in from a local fast-food place.*

69. VIDEO MEMORIES

SUPPLIES NEEDED: video camera, VHS tapes
COST: about $2 per person

You don't have to be a Hollywood producer to create a short video snapshot of the trip as a keepsake for each volunteer. Record some of the fun moments of the trip (or have a student do it for you). When adult volunteers aren't around, pull a few students aside and do some short video interviews. Ask them questions like: "What has been your favorite part of this trip?" "How has this trip impacted your faith?" or "How will your life at home change as a result of this trip?" And of course, prompt each student you interview to share a message of thanks to all the adult volunteers who helped make the trip happen.

When you get home, you may need to do some editing. Then duplicate the video, write "Thanks!" on the side of each tape, and give them to the volunteers at your next team meeting.

FILL THEIR TOOLBOX

A big source of discouragement among volunteers is the feeling that they are ill-equipped to handle much of what ministry throws their way: trying to lead seventh grade boys through a twenty-week study of Leviticus, spending a week at camp in a hot and stinky cabin full of students while the youth pastor lounges around alone in his air-conditioned suite, or dealing with a dad who is upset that "the Word doesn't get preached enough." (Apparently he doesn't know about the twenty-week study of Leviticus!) The list could, quite literally, go on and on!

Most volunteers haven't been to seminary. They probably haven't been to the latest and greatest training conferences. They may have never even been given a good book to read about ministry, and yet they're being asked to spend their time deeply embedded in hands-on student ministry.

Can you imagine someone who's interested in auto mechanics being tossed in front of a broken-down car with no training and an empty toolbox and being expected to repair the car? That's often what we do with our volunteers! They show an interest, and we toss them in front of a need, but we often fail to train them or fill their toolbox properly.

Don't assume that the new volunteer who has raised three great children knows how to engage other students in meaningful conversation...fill her toolbox! Just because he's young and athletic doesn't mean he understands relational ministry...fill his toolbox! She's been involved in your ministry for a long time and wants to take on some new roles...fill her toolbox!

How you fill their toolboxes is up to you. Have quarterly training meetings, loan them your ministry books, bring in an "expert" to share about certain topics, e-mail them links to relevant Web sites, or send them to a one-day seminar.

I've never met a mechanic who thought he had too many tools in his toolbox.

70. POST-TRIP FOLLOW-UP

SUPPLIES NEEDED: trip picture, printer-ready stationery
COST: under $2 per person

Don't forget the follow-up! Take a moment when you get back from your trip to write a thank-you note or an e-mail to all volunteers involved with your trip. Being away on a trip with students takes a lot of time and energy; the better the follow-up, the more likely they are to return on another trip with you. A cool way to do a follow-up thank-you card is to turn your camp picture into stationery. While you are away at camp, take a picture of all of your students and counselors together—one big group picture. Scan that picture onto fun printer-ready stationery, and write your thank-you note on that! It's a great keepsake and a cool way to say thank you from everyone.

Happy Holidays!

Greeting card companies have long been accused of inventing holidays for the sole purpose of selling more cards. If it's true, it's pure genius! Take advantage of the fact that there are lots of holidays every year, and use them as a fun excuse to energize your volunteers. There isn't a month on the calendar that doesn't have a traditional (or not-so-traditional) holiday you can celebrate.

71. January

Supplies Needed: New Year's party supply (such as a noisemaker, party hat, or party popper), note card, blank journal
Cost: under $5 per person

The start of a new year is always an exciting time in ministry. It's a time to set new goals, meet new students, and cast new vision. Ring in the new year with your volunteers! Start the year off with a little encouragement!

Send a party hat or a party popper with a note attached. Write, "We are so excited to have you as a part of the team this year!" Or send your volunteer a blank journal. Jot a little note on the first page to encourage your volunteer to set ministry and personal goals for the new year. For something extra, send your volunteers a book of devotions such as *Living the Beatitudes of Jesus* or *God Is Near* (both available from Group Publishing, Inc.) to help them grow spiritually.

72. February

Supplies Needed: red or pink construction paper or store-bought Valentine cards
Cost: varies

February—Valentine's Day—the month of love! What a great opportunity to remind your volunteers how much you love them and how much God loves them. Cheap Valentine cards cover the shelves in February. Go on a search in your favorite store, and pick out Valentine cards that suit your volunteers. Or have students make homemade, personalized Valentine cards. Be sure to include a verse from God's love letter!

Get some pink or red construction paper, and cut out a huge heart. In the center of the heart, write 1 Corinthians 13:4-7, "Love is patient, love is kind. It does not envy, it does not boast, it is not proud. It is not rude, it is not self-seeking, it is not easily angered, it keeps no record of wrongs. Love does not delight in evil but rejoices with the truth. It always protects, always trusts, always hopes, always perseveres." Then write a little note to your volunteer, "You are loved! Thank you for loving others."

73. MARCH

SUPPLIES NEEDED: something green, large envelope, postage
COST: under $5 per person

A day or two before St. Patrick's Day, mail volunteers something green just to let them know that you're looking out for them! A dorky green tie, a pair of green socks, a pair of green sunglasses—the possibilities are endless!

74. APRIL

SUPPLIES NEEDED: note card
COST: free

Create a twist on April Fools' Day. Celebrate the fact that your volunteers are involved in something that much of the world would view as foolish. Remind them that they are in great company! Scripture is full of men and women who look foolish in the eyes of others but did awesome things for God. Write a note thanking them for being foolish!

EXAMPLES
- *David fighting Goliath*
- *Noah building the ark*
- *Rahab hiding the twelve spies*
- *The Israelites marching around Jericho*
- *Peter and Andrew leaving their nets to follow Jesus*
- *Ananias showing kindness to Saul, the persecutor of Christians*

75. MAY

SUPPLIES NEEDED: varies
COST: under $10 per person

The month of May is a great opportunity for you to honor the moms serving in your volunteer ministry. Celebrate their ministry and their role as mothers by sending them a little encouragement. Below are some ways you could encourage the moms on your team.

EXAMPLES
- *Organize a lunch or a tea to celebrate Mother's Day. Have students serve lunch and play the role of host.*
- *Send each mom her favorite flowers.*
- *Send each mom a personalized Mother's Day card. Have all of the students in your ministry sign it.*
- *Honor the mothers in front of your students.*

76. JUNE

SUPPLIES NEEDED: a tie, note card or sticky label
COST: under $5 per person

June is the perfect opportunity to honor "Dad"—not just our earthly father but our heavenly Father too. Honor the dads on your volunteer team by sending them a small encouragement on Father's Day. Go to a local thrift store, and pick up a variety of old neckties. Attach a note or write directly on the front of the tie. Personalize each tie, honoring and encouraging each of the dads on your volunteer staff.

Another idea is to invite your volunteers to come to a worship night. Spend the evening singing, praying, and worshipping God, our Father. This could be an awesome encouragement for your volunteers to get re-connected to "Dad."

77. JULY

SUPPLIES NEEDED: varies
COST: varies

Host a "Freedom in Christ" party. Sometime around the Fourth of July, host a party to celebrate true freedom—the freedom that comes from serving Jesus Christ! Make it look and feel similar to a traditional American Fourth of July party, and ask one or two people to share the story of their own faith journey. End the evening in a time of prayer thanking God for the freedom he offers through Christ. Use John 8:36 as your theme verse: "So if the Son sets you free, you will be free indeed."

78. AUGUST

SUPPLIES NEEDED: beach ball, envelope or sticky label, postage
COST: under $2 per person

Write an encouragement note on a deflated beach ball. For example, "You are doing an awesome job serving students this summer! Thanks for all of your time! Take a break and hit the pool! Have a great week!" Stick it in an envelope, or stick enough postage right on the beach ball and send it to your volunteer!

79. SEPTEMBER

SUPPLIES NEEDED: ice cream gift certificate, note card
COST: under $5 per person

Send ice cream shop gift certificates and a note: "Cool off on us!"

80. OCTOBER

SUPPLIES NEEDED: large leaf, small paper tag with string
COST: free

When October comes around, fall has arrived. Send your volunteer a leaf with a note attached saying, "Thank you for your unique contribution to our ministry!"

TIP

Add "umph" to this idea by giving away mini-pumpkins instead of leaves. Attach notes to each mini-pumpkin, thanking the volunteers for being part of God's spiritual harvest.

81. NOVEMBER

SUPPLIES NEEDED: paper, pens
COST: free

Give each volunteer a homemade "10 Reasons I'm Thankful for You" card. Personalize it for each volunteer. Encourage students to do this for a specific volunteer who works with them.

EXAMPLE
1. I am thankful for your heart for students.
2. I am thankful for the role you play as small group leader.
3. I am thankful that you open your home for Bible study each week.
4. I am thankful for your family.
5. I am thankful for your sense of humor.

6. I am thankful that you share the love of Christ with others.

7. I am thankful for your commitment to serving.

8. I am thankful for you coming to camp as a counselor.

9. I am thankful for your support.

10. I am thankful to be a part of your life.

82. DECEMBER

SUPPLIES NEEDED: camera, film, paper, postage
COST: varies

Create and send out a "Year in Review" letter by taking pictures throughout the year of your volunteers and writing a letter to accompany the photos. Write about what God did in your ministry, put captions next to pictures of volunteers in action, and share with others in your church about how wonderful your volunteers are. Send the letters to your church staff, your volunteers and their families, students in your ministry, and families in the church body. Highlight the volunteers, and write about them like they were your family!

TOP 5 THINGS
THAT SOUND ENCOURAGING
BUT REALLY AREN'T

5. "For an old guy, you are a really good small group leader."

4. "The object lesson you shared almost made sense."

3. "Thanks for running camp; soon you'll be ready for some real responsibility."

2. "I can't put my finger on it, but for some reason students really like you."

1. "I haven't had a parent complain about you in days!"

EMPOWERING PARENTS TO ENERGIZE YOUR VOLUNTEERS

Parents are a powerful force! Youth workers often wonder how they can get parents more involved in the youth ministry. Many parents who want to be involved in some way often feel like they just don't have the time to volunteer as a Sunday school teacher, small group leader, or event coordinator. We have an answer! Use parents as a source of encouragement to the volunteers on your team. These ideas will help parents play a vital role in your ministry without requiring a big time commitment.

83. PARENT PRAYER

SUPPLIES NEEDED: none
COST: free

Motivate the parents in your ministry to support your volunteers through prayer. Parents want to be active, so what better way to get them involved than to partner them in prayer with a few volunteers in your ministry? Send out a weekly e-mail to parents with two volunteers they could pray for that week. Give specific requests and ideas for prayer. For example, if you have a volunteer who is really struggling with his or her small group Bible study, have parents pray specifically for the group. This is a great opportunity for parents to lift up volunteers and for volunteers to feel encouraged.

84. Cookie Mania

Supplies Needed: none
Cost: free

Give willing parents two volunteers to bake cookies for each month. Find out what each volunteer's favorite cookie is, and pass that along to families willing to bake them! Have parents hand deliver them or bring them to your next volunteer meeting. Tell parents to write an encouragement note and attach it to the plate of cookies. This is something extra that parents can do to make ministry a little sweeter.

85. Don't Call Us, We'll Call You!

Supplies Needed: none
Cost: free

A great way to get your ministry parents involved with serving your volunteers is to have them call two volunteers a month. Each month, gather parents who are willing to call, pray for, thank, and encourage your volunteers. It could be a message on the answering machine or a personal conversation. It's awesome for volunteers to hear "thank you" from the parents of the kids they are ministering to. Also, with the busy schedules of parents and families these days, calling two volunteers a month is an easy commitment!

86. Dear Counselor

Supplies Needed: none
Cost: free

After a long week at camp, ask parents to write a thank-you note to their child's counselor. It's a big commitment to serve as a counselor all week. A surprising but welcome encouragement for volunteers would be a personal thank-you card from the parents of the specific students they ministered to all week. Encourage parents to share any funny stories that their teenager told them or any spiritual commitments their child may have made during the week away.

EXAMPLE

Brittany,

Thank you so much for spending a week at camp with my daughter. You truly made an impact on her life! She told me about the water fight and staying up until midnight talking...she also told me about her decision to commit her life to Jesus Christ. Thank you for sharing your journey with her all week. She came home excited about her new faith!

—Dave

TEAM TALK

"We love serving together on our youth ministry team for three simple reasons: First, the leadership has made it convenient for us to serve as a married couple; second, we've built lasting friendships within the ministry team; and third, working together has allowed us to share each other's hardships, frustrations, praises, and successes...leading to a closer bond with each other and Jesus Christ."

—Mike and Vicki Zoradi
Serving together since 1997; extremely dedicated; very much in love

87. DINNER PARTY

SUPPLIES NEEDED: none
COST: varies

Find a parent willing to host an appreciation dinner party for your youth volunteers in his or her home. It's a great opportunity for your parents to "love on" volunteers face-to-face.

88. SECRET PAL

SUPPLIES NEEDED: none
COST: free

Give parents a "Secret Pal" on your volunteer staff for the school year. Assign one parent or a team of parents a specific volunteer to encourage throughout the school year. Keep it a secret just for fun.

Secret stuff parents can do:
- Send a card in the mail.
- Bring lunch to the volunteer's work. (Leave it at the front desk.)
- Send a gift certificate to the person's favorite store.
- Send a little something on holidays and birthdays.
- Tie a bunch of balloons onto the volunteer's car antenna.
- Leave an encouraging "mystery message" on the volunteer's answering machine.

89. SUBSTITUTE TEACHER

SUPPLIES NEEDED: none
COST: varies

Halfway through your year, encourage your volunteers by giving them a special treat at your weekly program. Have parents show up to your program ready to fill in as "substitute leaders." When your volunteers arrive, load them up in a van and take them out for pizza or ice cream or to a restaurant of their choice! It will be a nice break for your volunteers midyear, and it will give parents an opportunity to experience what the volunteers do each week in your ministry. This idea will foster appreciation from your volunteers *and* appreciation from your parents for what the volunteers do each week!

On the Same Side of the Rope

Unfortunately ministry often looks like a game of tug of war. The ministry becomes that little red flag in the center of the rope that is being pulled in opposite directions toward different goals. If you are the appointed leader of your ministry, your time is best spent doing the things that only you can do and empowering others to do the rest. One of the things that only you can do is to get everyone on the same side of the rope, pulling together toward the common goals you have determined are important.

Why does this ministry exist? What is our purpose? Who are we trying to reach? Why do we do what we do? These are just a few of the issues that tend to cause people to jump on their side of the rope and tug like crazy! If you haven't answered these questions, it may be time to take a day away and figure out the direction you want your ministry to go and then dedicate yourself to getting the rest of your team on board.

When everyone is on the same side of the rope, good things happen! Progress is made, goals are reached, and momentum is built. People with their own agendas who are still holding onto the other side of the rope are quickly pulled the direction the ministry is heading, or they let go of the rope altogether and find another department in the church to "tug against" for a while.

Tug of war makes a fun camp game: Both sides fight real hard until someone finally ends up defeated and muddy. It's probably not a game we want to play with our volunteers.

90. Cleanup Crew

Supplies Needed: none
Cost: free

The last thing your volunteers want to do when they arrive home from a trip with students is clean out the church van. It's inevitable that the vans will be a mess upon return to the church. Why not have parents meet you at the church when you return from a trip? Have parents clean out vans, clean up equipment, and help students gather all of their belongings. That way you can send your volunteers home as soon as they arrive back. It's a huge encouragement to volunteers to be able to go straight home to the families they have been away from for a few days!

Encouraging Rookies and Veterans

As your volunteer team grows, you will begin to have different types of volunteers serving in the trenches with you. On one hand, you could have volunteers who have been serving in ministry for ten years, and on the other hand, you could have volunteers who have been serving for ten days. Encouragement looks different for "rookies" and "veterans." Oftentimes a volunteer who is new to ministry is faced with different obstacles than a veteran who has been around for a while. In this section, check out encouragement ideas to meet the needs of the different types of volunteers in your ministry.

Rookies

91. First Call

Supplies Needed: none
Cost: free

The first few months of ministry can be a tough time for a "rookie" volunteer. It can be discouraging, draining, and full of surprises. For the first two months of a rookie's ministry, take time to call or e-mail him or her once a week. It gives you an opportunity to encourage, train, and guide that person in ministry, and it gives the volunteer the opportunity to ask questions, relay tough situations, and ask for prayer. It also gives both you and your volunteer some quality time to get to know each other!

Top 5 Things *Not* to Say to a Potential Volunteer

5. "So, is your health insurance paid up?"

4. "Eventually, you'll get used to the Sunday afternoon migraines."

3. "I know you'd like to mentor a high school senior, but we really need you to teach our seventh grade boys' Sunday school class."

2. "Wow that's a nice Hummer! Can the youth group have it?"

1. "By the way, can you teach for me tonight?"

---

92. Baseball Card

Supplies Needed: a piece of thin cardboard, a picture of your volunteer
Cost: free

A fun way to introduce new volunteers to your ministry is with a "Team Baseball Card." Make a baseball card with your volunteer's picture on the front, and on the back include fun "stats" about his or her life.

Example

Front of card:

Back of card:

Amanda Maguire
- Favorite food—pasta
- Favorite sport—football
- Married to Jeff—5/23/99
- 1 son—Dylan
- Loves camp, lock-ins, and leading small group Bible study

TEAM TALK

"My plan was to volunteer one week in Mexico on a youth mission trip to spend some time with my daughter. Five years later I'm still here, and my daughter is off to college. I'm fully entrenched in my ministry because of the every-day encouragement that I get from the leaders of our youth ministry. It's one of the reasons I've stayed connected. Katie has a unique way of making me feel special and necessary to this ministry."

–Mike Losey
Family man; opens his house to students;
at almost every ministry event; surfer

93. BAG O' MINISTRY FUN

SUPPLIES NEEDED: small bag, gift items
COST: under $10 per person

Create a ministry "Bag o' Fun" for your new volunteers. Fill it with all different types of tools that will help them be successful in their ministry. Sometimes when you are just starting out in youth ministry, you really don't know where to begin. Encourage your rookie volunteers by giving them a little head start!

Fill the bag with...
- a fun trivia or questions book (for discussions with students).
- fast-food gift certificates.
- an explanation of the youth ministry values and expectations.
- encouraging notes or tips from veteran volunteers.
- treats.
- a few funny things, like aspirin and adhesive bandages, for the "dangers" of ministry.

A Support System

Initially, it may be very easy to encourage and care for all the volunteers in your ministry, especially if the only volunteer also happens to be your spouse! However as time moves on and your ministry begins to grow, it may become more difficult to keep up. Oftentimes, as the number of volunteers increases, the amount of care given decreases tremendously. To avoid this, initiate some type of volunteer support system that will help ensure that each volunteer is being cared for on a regular basis. Here are two simple ideas:

• **Coaches**—Ask certain volunteers to be coaches who, in essence, provide the encouragement and care for a group of volunteers on your behalf. You encourage and care for the coaches, and they each do the same for five or six volunteers of their own. This helps ensure that nobody slips through the cracks and that even when you aren't around, volunteers are still getting the care they need.

• **Cards**—Create a large index card for each volunteer, and write down the information you decide you must know about each one. Refer to this card as you write a note or speak on the phone. Use the card to jot down stuff that comes up in conversation so you can refer to it later. The card can serve as a great way to remember the "biggies" in each volunteer's life. Here are a few things you might put on the card: birthday, anniversary, spouse and/or children's names, place of employment, and favorite snack. Be sure to use pencil since some of the information may change as the volunteers stay for the long haul.

VETERANS

94. THE GOLDEN RULE

SUPPLIES NEEDED: small ruler, small paper tag
COST: under $2 per person

Longevity is not very common in youth ministry. That is why it is very important to take time out to encourage and uplift volunteers who have been "in the trenches" for a number of years. One unique way to encourage a veteran is to give him or her a ruler with a note attached, saying, "There's no way to measure the impact you've had on our ministry." It's just something little, but it will go a long way with your volunteer. (For extra impact, consider giving your volunteer a yardstick or even a tape measure!)

95. HAPPY ANNIVERSARY!
SUPPLIES NEEDED: varies
COST: varies

Celebrate ministry anniversaries! When you have a veteran volunteer who hits a milestone in his or her ministry, take time to honor that person in front of students and fellow volunteers. Create an appreciation tradition that honors veteran volunteers every five years.

Tradition ideas:
- five years—a small Bible engraved with the person's name and the name of the church or youth ministry
- ten years—a watch or a bracelet engraved with "Thank you"
- fifteen years—a framed collage of pictures from all years of the person's ministry, and an overnight getaway for the volunteer and his or her spouse
- twenty years—a dinner in the volunteer's honor with attendees (old students, parents, and fellow volunteers) who have been impacted by his or her ministry

QUALITY TIME

Over the years, there have likely been countless activities that you and your volunteers have been involved in. Most of those activities involve being with students or doing ministry. Why not take time out together and have some fun as a team? Spend some quality time getting to know each of your volunteers outside of the youth ministry circle. Meet their families, spend time laughing, and share life.

96. VOLUNTEER RETREAT

SUPPLIES NEEDED: varies
COST: varies

Plan an annual "Volunteer Retreat" to bond as a team, refresh spirits, get to know one another better, set goals, have fun, and renew hearts. Encourage your volunteers by spending quality time away with them. No students, no programs, no parents, no work...just get away and spend time together!

Volunteer Retreat Sample Agenda

Saturday

9:00 a.m.—Meet at church

11:00 a.m.—Arrive at hotel

1:00 p.m.—Golf, shop, or see movie

5:00 p.m.—Dinner together at a restaurant

7:00 p.m.—Meet together

- Praise and worship
- Sharing and praying for one another
- Devotion

9:00 p.m.—Late-night dessert run

Sunday

    9:00 a.m.—Breakfast together

    10:00 a.m.—Meet together

- Talk about ministry vision.
- Set personal ministry goals and share them with each other.
- Pray for our ministry.

    Noon—Lunch together, go home

Retreat Location Ideas
- beach house
- hotel in a fun area
- someone's vacation home
- church
- home/hotel in the mountains
- campground

Retreat Checklist

☐ Call around to different hotels. Be sure to ask for a group rate. Also, ask about any special promotions or offers the hotel might have.

☐ Make dinner reservations for the group.

☐ Call around to see what kind of activities are in the area (such as a baseball field, movie theaters, dessert options, bowling, or shopping).

☐ Make a promotional flier for your volunteers, highlighting the times, dates, costs, and location.

---

97. FUN NIGHT OUT

SUPPLIES NEEDED: varies
COST: varies

The team that plays together stays together! Schedule a Fun Night Out three or four times a year for your volunteer team. In our ministry, we like to have a fun night out every time a month has a fifth Sunday night. Invite families, invite spouses, and get creative. And since you are calling it Fun Night Out, be sure to have lots of it!

Fun Night Out ideas:
- Meet at a local pizza parlor for dinner.
- Go miniature golfing.
- Go bowling.
- Go roller-skating or ice-skating.
- Meet at someone's house for dinner.
- Watch a sporting event together.
- Meet for lunch after church one week.
- Organize a Sports Day.
- Rent a classic movie from your junior high or high school years.

TIP

Be sure to make it as inexpensive as possible. If one of your volunteers is bringing his or her whole family, it could end up being a pricey night!

Also, consider asking a generous parent or leader in your church to donate funds to underwrite the cost of these events.

Armed With Fun

Youth ministry is serious stuff! The world has changed quite a bit since those of us who lead a youth group were actually in one ourselves. It sometimes feels like every time we step foot into our youth ministry, we are entering a battlefield: a battlefield for morality, a battlefield for right choices, a battlefield for truth.

Years ago, Bob Hope made his mark in America's history by providing skits, comedy, and music to U.S. soldiers stationed overseas. He'd show up on the scene and provide an outlet of fun in a very serious setting.

As the leader of a ministry, you want your volunteer troops to be well prepared. I hope you are equipping them, training them, and keeping them ready for battle. I also hope you are having fun! I'm no Bob Hope, but I do understand the power that fun and laughter can bring to any environment. When's the last time you laughed at yourself or gave others the freedom to laugh at you? Did you include any comic relief during your latest training session? Have you ever taken your volunteer team out for a night of pizza and Go Kart racing?

Take youth ministry seriously. Understand that the stakes are high. Equip your troops well, but don't forget to be armed with fun.

98. KIDS' STUFF
SUPPLIES NEEDED: varies
COST: varies

Plan an entire night to do all the fun stuff you do with students...but don't invite them! So often your volunteers spend their ministry time organizing and leading the fun stuff that they don't get to enjoy it themselves. Pick some of your youth group's favorite activities.

EXAMPLES
- *Toilet paper your senior pastor's house.*
- *Have a night of silly relays.*

TEAM TALK

"Volunteering in youth ministry has been one of God's greatest gifts. Helping deliver *real truth* in a fun and fresh way with leaders who encourage, exhort, and care for me continues to fuel my sense of fulfillment and purpose. I totally love it!"

—Gary Eilts
Junior high volunteer for over fifteen years

99. YEAR-END PARTY
SUPPLIES NEEDED: varies
COST: varies

At the end of the year, host a party to celebrate another year of ministry and to thank your team for all of their hard work. Be sure to include various highlights of the past year.

EXAMPLES

- *Show a slide show highlighting the year in review.*
- *Ask several students to share how they've grown in the past year because of your leaders' influence.*
- *Hand out a list of accomplishments. Include some funny stuff.*
  - *number of first-time guests*
  - *total number of students who came through your doors*
  - *number of lives touched through service projects*
  - *number of injuries that required medical attention*
  - *number of rental van miles logged*

100. FUN GUY STUFF

SUPPLIES NEEDED: varies
COST: varies

Host an event just for the guys. Try one of these ideas:
- Host a Macho Movies night, and show an action movie.
- Hold a barbecue at a local park and play softball, horseshoes, or basketball.
- Have a video game night at someone's house.
- Take a night and do your own version of *Monster Garage* or *Trading Spaces.*

101. Fun Girl Stuff

Supplies Needed: varies

Cost: varies

Plan an event just for your female volunteers. How about these ideas?
- Plan a Girls' Day Out.
- Show up at your weekly meeting with a flower for each female volunteer.
- Start a Bible study for your female volunteers.
- Host an annual tea party for your female staff.
- Go ice-skating, bowling, or mountain-biking.
- Plan a game night with fun prizes.
- Find a cosmetic line that is willing to donate free products.

Top 5 Signs a Volunteer May Not Need Any Extra Encouragement

5. The town already holds a parade in her honor every year.

4. Students in your youth group are wearing shirts with his picture on the front.

3. He has his own action figure at Toys"R"Us.

2. The phrase "What Would Jesus Do?" has been replaced by "What Would Sue Do?"

1. CNN reports that his image is being added to Mount Rushmore.

EVALUATION FOR
Go Team!

Please help Group Publishing, Inc., continue to provide innovative and useful resources for ministry. Please take a moment to fill out this evaluation and mail or fax it to us. Thanks!

Group Publishing, Inc.
Attention: Product Development
P.O. Box 481
Loveland, CO 80539
Fax: (970) 292-4370

1. As a whole, this book has been (circle one)

not very helpful   very helpful

  1   2   3   4   5   6   7   8   9   10

2. The best things about this book:

3. Ways this book could be improved:

4. Things I will change because of this book:

5. Other books I'd like to see Group publish in the future:

6. Would you be interested in field-testing future Group products and giving us your feedback? If so, please fill in the information below:

Name_____

Church Name _____

Denomination _____ Church Size _____

Church Address _____

City _____ State_____ ZIP _____

Church Phone _____

E-mail _____